This Book Donated By

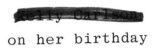

on her birthday

©Highsmith Inc. 1999

Galloping across the USA
Horses in American Life

Transportation in America

Galloping across the USA
Horses in American Life

Martin W. Sandler

OXFORD
UNIVERSITY PRESS

This book is dedicated to the staff of the Osterville, Massachusetts Public Library in appreciation of all the help they have given me, and to librarians across the country for their dedication in fostering the love of books in children.

Acknowledgments

I wish to thank Carol Sandler for all the help and encouragement she has given me. Thanks are also due to Steve Wilson for his valuable suggestions and to Alexis Siroc for the appealing design of the book. Finally, I am grateful for having Karen Fein as my editor. Her editing skills are but part of the many contributions she has made to both this book and the series.

Picture Credits

Butler Institute of American Art: 24; City of Boston Mounted Police Unit: 57; Gilcrease Institute: 7; Kansas State Historical Society: 23; Library of Congress: 8, 11, 14, 16, 17, 20, 22, 25, 27, 28, 31, 33, 34, 38, 41, 43, 45, 46, 48, 50, 51, 53, 54; Maryland Historical Society: 18; National Archives (NWDNS-57-HS-895): 29; National Museum of the American Indian: 9; Naylor Collection: 39; New York City Mounted Police Unit: 56; Sandler Collection: 55.

OXFORD
UNIVERSITY PRESS

Oxford   New York

Auckland   Bangkok   Buenos Aires   Cape Town   Chennai
Dar es Salaam   Delhi   Hong Kong   Istanbul   Karachi   Kolkata
Kuala Lumpur   Madrid   Melbourne   Mexico City   Mumbai   Nairobi
São Paulo   Shanghai   Singapore   Taipei   Tokyo   Toronto

Copyright © 2003 by Martin W. Sandler

Design by Alexis Siroc

Published by Oxford University Press, Inc.
198 Madison Avenue, New York, New York, 10016
http://www.oup-usa.org

Oxford is a registered trademark of Oxford University Press

Library of Congress Cataloging-in-Publication Data

Sandler, Martin W.
  Galloping across the USA : horses in American life / Martin W. Sandler.
     p. cm. — (Transportation in America)
  Includes bibliographical references and index.
    ISBN 0-19-513226-2 (alk. paper)
  1. Horses—United States—History. 2. Draft horses—United States—History. 3. Horse-drawn vehicles—United States—History. I. Title. II. Series.
  SF284.U5 S26 2003
  636.1'00973—dc21   2002012414

9 8 7 6 5 4 3 2 1

Printed in Hong Kong on acid-free paper

ON THE COVER: **A 19th-century winter scene with four horse-drawn sleighs by American artist Joseph Hoover.**

FRONTISPIECE: **Frontier farmers with teams of tens of horses pulling harvesting equipment.**

Contents

CHAPTER 1

Conquistadores and Prairie Warriors

"A white man will ride the mustang until he is played out; a Mexican will take him and ride him, and ride him another day until he thinks he is played out; a Comanche will mount him, and ride him to where he is going."

—J. Frank Dobie, in *The Southwest Review,* 1911

The story of transportation in America is the saga of a people constantly on the move. It is also the story of the continual search to find new and better ways to transport people and goods as dependably and as fast as possible. This story begins with the horse.

Horses have been companions to humans since long before written history. Archaeologists and scientists have determined that some form of horses inhabited the earth as far back as 54 million years ago, and they existed in North America 8 to 10 thousand years ago. At some time in that period, however, horses became extinct.

In the late 15th and early 16th centuries, the Spanish reintroduced horses to America. Christopher Columbus took the first ones to the Caribbean in 1492. Spanish explorer Hernán Cortés transported the first horses to the North American mainland in 1519. In the years that followed, other Spanish explorers and military men known as conquistadores brought countless other horses with them to America.

The conquistadores had come to the New World in search of vast riches reportedly possessed by its natives, who had lived there for tens of thousands of years.

An Indian boy's years of riding lessons included learning to cross a river on horseback.

The Spaniards relied heavily on their horses not only to transport themselves in their search for plunder but also as a unique weapon against the Native Americans (or Indians, as Columbus named them). They knew that the Indians had never seen men mounted high atop horses before and that the sight would terrorize them. "Horses," stated one conquistador, "are what the Indians dread most, and by means of which they will be overcome."

The conquistadores did succeed in conquering many of the Native North Americans. But they never found the cities of gold and jewels that they sought.

When they left the New World, their horses—which had multiplied—remained. Particularly in the American Southwest and on the Great Plains, these animals would change the Indians' manner of living in ways that they could never have imagined.

The Spanish called the horses they had introduced into the New World *mesteños,* meaning "wild." In America they became known as mustangs. Descended from several breeds, most notably Arabians, mustangs possessed endurance, strength, and swiftness—qualities perfectly suited for a hard life on the rugged terrain.

Before they had horses, most of the southwestern and Plains Indians sustained themselves by farming, fishing, hunting on foot, or by gathering roots, tubers, and seeds. The horse changed all that by making it possible for the Native Americans to pursue the buffalo. Before the arrival of the horse, Native Americans captured buffalo by driving them over cliffs or steep banks called "buffalo jumps." Now, Indians could hunt buffalo anywhere.

Indians use their horses as shields in a confrontation with settlers. The Plains Indians developed skills that would earn them the reputation of being among the most accomplished horsemen in the world.

Limited only by severe weather or by territory occupied by more powerful rival tribes, Indians followed the buffalo wherever the herds sought pasture. One skilled man on horseback could, in a single buffalo hunt, provide his family with enough meat to last for weeks. In addition, various parts of the flesh, skin, and bones of the buffalo supplied the tribes with clothing, tools, bedding, glue, fuel, and drink. The hides of these animals proved to be the perfect covering for tepees, in which many Indians lived.

Not only did horses allow Native Americans to pursue and hunt down buffalo, and to travel greater distances than ever before, but the horses themselves became valuable. As the horse became increasingly important to the Native American way of life, an Indian's wealth and social standing came to be measured by the number of horses he owned.

Driven by the desire to acquire as many animals as they could, many tribes began raiding Spanish settlements or other tribes that owned large numbers of horses. Tribes on horseback also battled each other for

Once they had horses, as this Crow Indian painting on elk skin reveals, the Plains Indians made buffalo hunting a way of life.

possession of favored buffalo hunting grounds. During these raids and skirmishes it became evident that, thanks to the horse and their remarkable riding skills, the Indians had become formidable warriors. The Plains Indians would demonstrate their prowess throughout their historic battles for survival against the U.S. cavalry during the 1870s and 1880s. In these battles the Plains Indians practiced some of the most remarkable feats on horseback ever witnessed in America.

Years after the cavalry's superior numbers and weapons had driven Indians from their lands, General Randolph B. Marcy, who had spent many years in the West, would attest to the Native Americans' equestrian skills. "It is when mounted that the prairie warrior exhibits himself to the best advantage," he said.

Here he is at home, and his skill in various maneuvers which he makes available in battle such as throwing himself entirely upon the side of his horse and discharging his arrows with great rapidity toward the opposite side from beneath the animal's neck while he is at full speed is truly astonishing…every warrior has his war-horse, which is the fleetest that can be obtained, and he prizes him more highly than anything else in his possession, and it is seldom that he can be induced to part with him at any price.

Given all that the horse enabled Native Americans to do, it is not surprising that the animal was their most prized possession. In many tribes, when an Indian died, his favorite horse was shot at the grave—a testimony to a way of life in which Native Americans had become profoundly linked to their horses.

Seven Navajo Indians ride in Arizona's Canyon de Chelly in the early 1900s in this picture by photographer Edward Curtis.

CHAPTER 2

The Horse Pulls the Load

"If there is a prettier sight of animation than a Concord coach with six spirited horses in bright harness, and a good reinsman on the box, we have not seen it yet."

—*Boston Post*, 1841

The Spanish brought horses to the New World to aid them in their search for riches. During the 1600s and 1700s, colonists from such nations as England, France, Holland, and Sweden arrived with thousands more horses. In the beginning, the colonies depended upon the ships that sailed across the Atlantic from Europe to bring them many of the goods they needed.

As soon as the War of Independence was over and a new nation called the United States had been created, tall-masted American sailing ships were making their way across the Atlantic Ocean. Within the new nation

itself, various types of vessels transported people and goods along the eastern coastline, across the country's many lakes, and down its rivers.

Travel on land, however, was more difficult. The infant United States contained some 4 million people spread out over almost 800,000 square miles. Contact and communication between citizens and officials in each of the new states was essential if the new nation was to survive. The problem was that there were almost no adequate roads. The few roads that did make their way through the dense forests of the eastern landscape were, for the most part, too narrow and often too bumpy to allow for the use of horse-drawn vehicles. In bad weather, they were totally impassable. Almost all overland travel, conducted on horseback, was exceedingly slow. When, for example, the Declaration of Independence was announced in Philadelphia and riders were dispatched to "quickly" inform the various colonies, it took 29 days for the news to reach South Carolina.

Overland travel was a serious problem, one that was not adequately addressed until some 20 years after the United States had been created. The answer came in the form of a type of road that had first appeared in medieval England but had never been seen in America. It was called a turnpike, deriving its name from the pole (or pike) that stretched across the road at 10-mile intervals. At each of these barriers, travelers were required to pay a toll in order to continue on the road.

Turnpikes were constructed on a firm bed of different layers of crushed stones, which provided drainage and eliminated many of the problems of bad-weather travel. These roads were wide enough for even the

A trainer rubs down a horse's foreleg in this 1866 advertisement for horse liniment.

The passengers on this stagecoach in western Virginia are probably in for a rough ride and not even sure that the stage will reach its final destination. The few roads that did exist in the early the 1800s were bumpy and commonly turned into mud during rainy periods.

largest horse-drawn vehicles. Private road-building companies quickly learned that in a nation of people always eager to be on the move, such roads would attract thousands of travelers and would turn a hefty profit through the tolls that were collected.

By 1820 turnpikes had been built or were being constructed throughout the new nation. They became filled with travelers who marveled at the condition of the new roads. They were particularly delighted with the reduction in travel time. The 62-mile journey by horse and wagon from Lancaster, Pennsylvania (America's largest inland city), to Philadelphia, for example, had always taken more than a week. By using the Lancaster Turnpike, a farmer could make the trip in fewer than four days.

As tens of thousands of horses transported people and goods over the turnpikes from as far north as Boston to as far south as Georgia, observers remarked on the incredible turnaround in overland transportation. "To give an idea of the internal movements of this vast hive," wrote an English visitor,

about twelve thousand wagons passed from Baltimore and Philadelphia in the last year, with four to six horses. . . . Add to this . . . the innumerable travelers on horseback, on foot, and in light wagons, and you have before you a scene of bustle and business extending over a space of three hundred miles, which is truly wonderful.

The road-building boom did not stop with the turnpikes. Aware of the increased number of citizens moving westward through the Allegheny Mountains, the U.S. government began construction of a major thoroughfare through the rugged terrain. The first section of what came to be called the National Road ran from Cumberland, Maryland, to the western border of Ohio. Other sections were added until the road extended all the way to Vandalia, Illinois. As each section of the road was built, it became busy with early pioneers seeking new opportunities far away from the eastern communities. The National Road, wrote one early observer, "looked more like a leading avenue of a great city than a road through rural districts."

STEAMBOAT LINE.

STAGE NOTICE
FARE REDUCED!
COHASSET, SCITUATE & THE GLADES

On and after Tuesday, June 28th,

A STAGE will leave **COHASSET** for **HINGHAM**, connecting with Steamer Nantasket for **BOSTON**, at 6:30 & 9:45 A. M. and 3:30 P. M.

Leave **BOSTON** at 9 A. M., 2:30 & 6:00 P. M.

FARE THROUGH, FROM COHASSET TO BOSTON, 35 CENTS.

The proprietors of the South Shore House will run a Carriage to meet every Stage to and from Boston.

FARE THROUGH, FROM SCITUATE HARBOR TO BOSTON, 60 CENTS.

GRAY'S CORNER, 55 CENTS.
GANNETT'S " 50 "

Capt. **HENRY SYLVESTER** will be in readiness with his boat on the arrival of each Stage, to convey passengers to and from the Glades House.

Fare through from **BOSTON** to the **GLADES**, 60 Cents.

J. W. RICHARDSON.
JAMES BEAL.

COHASSET, JUNE 28, 1859.

The Massachusetts stagecoach line advertised here brought passengers to Scituate Harbor, where they could board a waiting steamboat for Boston.

As American roads continued to grow in number and improve, horse-drawn vehicles—ranging from one-horse shays and carriages to heavy freight wagons—dominated the thoroughfares. Two particular types of horse-drawn vehicles, however, were the most important in moving people and goods across the young nation. One was the Conestoga wagon; the other was the stagecoach.

The Conestoga wagon got its name from Pennsylvania's Conestoga River Valley. There, wagon makers had succeeded in constructing a vehicle so effective in hauling huge loads of farmers' products and other freight that it would become the main vehicle for heavy trucking along the National Road, the turnpikes, and the nation's many other new roads.

The way in which its bottom curved upward both in the front and the rear distinguished the Conestoga from other wagons. This innovation permitted a heavy load to be carried without danger of it shifting or spilling out, even when traveling along the bumpiest of roads. Because they were much sturdier than the wheels found on most other types of wagons, a Conestoga wagon's huge, iron-rimmed wheels allowed a driver to cover long distances over the roughest terrain.

A Conestoga wagon was as attractive as it was practical. Its underbody was always painted a vivid shade of blue. Its upper woodwork was a bright red. Rising up from the wagon's side boards were seven or eight wooden arcs over which white cloth was often slung as protection against searing sun or foul weather.

A team of four to six powerful horses, specially bred for the purpose, typically pulled Conestoga wagons. These horses were a highly mixed breed of several different types of sturdy workhorses, many of which European settlers had introduced to America.

Like the wagon it pulled, a team of Conestoga horses was an impressive sight. Carefully matched, the enormous animals marched ahead almost as one. Those who owned them took pride in the animals, which were groomed meticulously. Their reins were brightly colored. Clusters of large bells adorned wide, shiny harnesses made of the finest leather.

In addition to revolutionizing the transport of goods, the Conestoga wagon played another important role in American history. Because the head horse in the team that pulled a Conestoga was positioned on the left, the wagon driver would walk or ride on the left. Thus if he needed to pass someone he would pass them on the left and drive on the right side of the road. This is how the custom of driving on the right side of the road began in the United States.

The Conestoga wagon was created to move goods, not passengers, and it served this purpose better than any other horse-drawn vehicle of its time. Before its days were over, however, it would become even more celebrated for taking thousands of pioneers on the long journey deep into the American West. The stagecoach, on the other hand, was built specifically to carry passengers and to transport them with as much speed as possible.

Stagecoach lines had been established in the American colonies before the Revolution. Due to the bad road conditions and the primitive nature of the

A party of settlers heading West, their Conestoga wagons loaded with provisions, stop for refreshment at an inn near Baltimore. As horsedrawn traffic continually increased on the National Road, so were more and more inns built along the thoroughfare.

coaches themselves, journeys on these lines were at best terribly uncomfortable and at worst dangerous. The constant bouncing around had passengers so shaken up that many had trouble standing at journey's end. Many others were injured or even killed when the horses pulling the coach suddenly fell into a mud hole or plunged over an unexpected ridge or gully. The turnpikes, the National Road, and the expanding network of other thoroughfares changed things dramatically.

In the 1790s, for example, Congressman Josiah Quincy had traveled from Boston to Washington in his own horse-drawn coach. It took him a month to make the 400-mile trip. In 1826, Quincy made the same journey on a stagecoach line. The trip was completed in eight days.

To public officials like Quincy, and to many private citizens as well, the benefits of the stagecoach went beyond improved efficiency in travel. Faster, better transportation eased the long-held fear that the new nation would remain a scattered collection of isolated communities. "Now," reported a Boston newspaper,

> we have more than 70 different lines of 4- and 6-horse stages which regularly depart from the city in every direction. . . . If this species of improvement continues to advance with the same gigantic strides (and we see nothing to prevent), the time cannot be far distant when a complete consolidation of the interests and feelings of the people of the United States will be brought about.

From the 1830s on, a typical stagecoach contained three long seats, each accommodating three travelers. The people who sat on the front seat faced the back of the coach. Those who sat on the other seats faced the spirited team of four or six horses that pulled the vehicle. There was room for another passenger outside the coach next to the driver, a spot usually reserved for the most distinguished member of the traveling party. Small baggage was placed underneath the seats, and larger items were stowed in a space at the rear called the "boot." Portraits of famous Americans like George Washington or Benjamin Franklin adorned the sides of many stagecoaches; other coaches featured landscapes.

Over the years, various types of stagecoaches were built. The most successful one was called the Concord coach, built in Concord, New Hampshire. Usually painted a bright red, the Concord was made of the best wood, leather, iron, and brass available. It had an oval-shaped body with a suspension system that made it more comfortable to ride in than any other coach. Throughout the East, and later in the West, the Concord coach became one of the most popular of all horse-drawn vehicles. "If there is a prettier sight of animation than a red Concord Coach, with six spirited horses in bright harness, and a good reinsman on the box, we have not seen it yet," exclaimed the *Boston Post*. By the 1840s, stagecoach lines were running on regular schedules throughout the East. The U.S. Post

In Conestoga wagons and on horseback, pioneers make their way along the Oregon Trail, shepherding their sheep and cows as they go.

along the Mississippi. People would pour onto the road, anxious to discover what passengers were aboard and what mail was arriving.

The stagecoach had brought the people of the East closer together, but its role in helping to build and unify a nation was far from over. Both the stagecoach and the Conestoga wagon would play a part in the challenges and adventures that lay ahead in the West.

Office had begun paying subsidies to many of the lines in return for their carrying mail along with passengers. The sound of a horn, signaling the arrival of a stage at either a country post office or a village inn, had the same effect as the blast of a steamboat whistle in towns

CHAPTER 3

Settling the West

"[One sees] an almost unbroken stream of horses and emigrants from horizon to horizon…teams and covered wagons, horsemen…an endless stream of hardy, optimistic folk, going West to seek their fortunes and to settle an empire."

—James H. Kyner, Oregon railroad worker,
in a letter to his family, 1867

Almost from the moment the colonies won their independence from England, many Americans believed that it was only a matter of time before the vast western lands would be settled and the United States would stretch from coast to coast. Politicians, convinced that the restless citizens of a new nation were bound to seek opportunities in the West, even gave this belief a name. They called it Manifest Destiny.

The men, women, and children who were among the first to settle the West were a special breed. They possessed the courage and daring required to endure the hardships of a long, difficult journey, to conquer a wilderness, and to build new lives far away from those they left behind. Fortunately, most of them also possessed horses. These animals were indispensable both in getting the pioneers to the new territories and, once there, in helping them survive and prosper.

Between 1840 and 1870, thousands of families made the arduous and often dangerous journey to unfamiliar destinations, some 2,000 miles away. Many wanted to escape eastern cities that were already becoming overcrowded. Others were fleeing from the

Some of the wagon trains that brought settlers to the West were as long as a third of a mile. The editor of the popular newspaper *Republican* wrote that the sight reminded him "of the caravans described in the Bible."

low wages and horrible conditions they encountered working in factories. All were determined to start a new life on land they could call their own.

Some of these pioneers journeyed at least part of the way in stagecoaches and early railroad trains. The vast majority, however, were determined to take as many possessions as possible in order to set up homes and farm their new land, and so they journeyed the entire distance in wagons covered by canvas to protect their heavy loads. These covered wagons were of every size and shape. Thousands were Conestogas, which had already proved to be effective freight-hauling vehicles. Teams of six to eight horses drew some of the wagons. Others were hitched to a simple team of two horses.

No matter what type of wagon they used, almost none of the families dared to make the journey alone. Instead, they traveled in caravans, or wagon trains as they were called, ranging from a few vehicles to several hundred. The jumping-off place for these caravans was any one of a number of communities along the Missouri River, most notably the Missouri towns of

Independence, Council Bluffs, and St. Joseph. At each of these places, the families that would make up the wagon train hired an experienced leader, called a wagon boss, to lead the caravan all along its route.

One of the main responsibilities of the wagon boss was to select the trail they would follow to the West. There were several, but the most popular was the Oregon Trail. Like the other routes, it was a trail in name only. In reality, it was little more than a pair of wheel ruts made by the earliest wagons traveling west. The first 500 miles of the journey took the pioneers across the open lands and often dangerous rivers of the Great Plains to the foothills of the Rocky Mountains. Those determined to travel on to Oregon and California had to make their way over the high mountains and across the wide, empty deserts before reaching their destination.

Almost all the wagon trains started out in late April or early May. Leaving earlier meant arriving deep on the prairie before there was enough spring grass to feed the horses and other livestock. Starting later meant running the risk of being stranded because of early blizzards in the western mountains.

The journey from the Missouri River towns to the far western lands took as long as six months. The goal of each wagon boss was to cover at least 15 miles a day. The horses hauled the wagons at a slow, steady pace. Typically, the mother and younger children rode aboard the wagon while the father and older children

Immigrants in Kansas stop for a plain meal. "What to take and what to leave behind was the problem," wrote one pioneer wife. "Many of our most cherished treasures had to be left to give place to the more necessary articles."

With a schoolbook in her right hand and a telegraph cable in her left, a figure representing American progress leads a stagecoach, a covered wagon, and people on horseback westward in the late 1800s.

Galloping across the USA

rode alongside on horseback. There were many cases in which fathers and older sons made the entire journey walking beside the wagon because the families could not afford enough horses.

Caravans of covered wagons continually crossed the vast, open plains. In 1863 one of these caravans was made up of 900 wagons. A year later, more than 8,000 wagon trains passed through Omaha, Nebraska, in a single week. From a distance, the swaying wagons, their canvas tops billowing in the wind, looked like ships. Observers referred to them as prairie schooners.

They made a romantic sight, but for those making the journey, the trip was anything but romantic. Traveling such a long distance over primitive trails and often rugged terrain exacted a heavy toll on the wagons. Axles broke and wheels fell off, and they had to be repaired or replaced on the spot.

The toll on the horses and the humans was even greater. Many of even the sturdiest horses broke down under the strain of hauling the heavy wagons for so long. The trails were littered with the prized posses-sions of families who had to abandon their things in order to lighten the load so that the horses could plod on. Carcasses of horses that did not survive were also scattered along the trails.

Families traveling with children faced particular challenges. Youngsters sometimes got lost in the confu-sion as hundreds of wagons and families got ready to start up after pausing for an evening's rest. Many chil-dren fell off the moving wagons and were injured or even killed. Sickness among adults and children alike was common and spread rapidly through families trav-eling so closely together.

One of the greatest dangers came as a result of the ever-present temptation to find a shortcut. Rumors of a new, shorter trail or a cutoff sometimes lured one or more families into splitting off from the wagon train in the hope of shortening the journey. In most cases it was a disastrous decision. Most of the supposed new routes went in the wrong direction. Many families became so lost that they had to retrace their steps and find their way back to the main trail. Such detours delayed some for so long that, with food running out and the wagon train now far ahead of them, they had to abandon their dream and return to the East. Moving away from the wagon trains also put a lone family in danger of Indian attacks, although such attacks were rare. Without the support of the other members of a wagon train, one family's chances of surviving such an assault were small.

Despite all the hardships, however, the vast majority of pioneers succeeded in fulfilling the first part of their dream and arrived safely in the West. Whether they chose to settle somewhere on the Great Plains or in Oregon, California, or surrounding areas, all were aware that they now faced the perhaps greater challenge of surviving in an unfamiliar land.

By May of 1862 the U.S. government, intent on encouraging settlement of the West, had succeeded in passing the Homestead Act. It stated that any man or

By the 1880s, thanks to enormous horse-drawn harvester/threshers such as this one, a farmer could harvest more than 45 acres in a day. In the 1850s, it had taken a farmer more than two days to harvest one acre.

woman at least 21 years old, a citizen of the United States, and the head of a family could get 160 acres of federal land for a nominal fee of $10. The only requirement was that the settler live on the land for at least five years and make improvements upon it. Making improvements meant farming the land, and this is how the great majority of pioneers helped build more than half the nation.

The horse was vital in helping families farm their new land, which was different from any they had encountered. The prairie was covered with thick, deep-rooted grass that required a real effort to plow under. But the soil under the grass was among the richest in the world. And as early as the 1840s, western pioneers had, with the aid of their horses and simple plows, begun to till the land with crops. "You can behold the vast plain of

Published in 1876 for the centennial of Independence, this lithograph honors the farmers who, with the aid of their horses, fed the United States. The stalks of corn and sheaves of wheat in the corners of the central frame celebrate the plenty of the American West.

twelve thousand acres, all waving in golden color. . . . At this moment every man and boy and even women are actively engaged in cradling, raking, binding, and shocking [gathering] the golden harvest," wrote a Michigan farmer.

Soon, new farm machinery made their backbreaking labors easier and more productive. One of the first of these machines was the mechanical reaper, invented by Cyrus McCormick. Described as a "cross between a flying machine, a wheel barrow and a . . . chariot," the heavy mechanical reaper, drawn across the prairie by teams of as many as 20 horses, immediately cut the cost and labor of harvesting crops by more than a third.

In 1858, the harvester made it possible to quickly tie together the crops once they had been reaped, which increased the speed of gathering the crops even further. "The saucy machine has driven the scythe from the field," wrote the editor of a Philadelphia newspaper, "and the principal work of the harvest, now, is to drive the horse about the field a few times and lo!, the harvest is gathered."

Other machinery, such as mechanical plows, planters, and threshers, rapidly increased both farm productivity and the demand for horses. In 1849 western farmers grew and harvested 85,000,000 bushels of wheat. In 1890 that figure grew to 425,000,000 bushels. By that time, the produce of America's western farmlands was feeding most of the nation and a considerable part of the world.

Eventually, steam-driven tractors would take over the task of hauling the farm machinery. But the horse had led the way. And many western farmers continued to use horses to work the fields until the late 1920s and early 1930s.

Delayed by Buffalo

"We saw them in frightful droves as far as the eye could reach, appearing at a distance as if the ground itself was moving like a sea," wrote pioneer John Wyeth in a letter to relatives back East. For many pioneers the most remarkable sight was the enormous herds of buffalo that roamed the American plains. "Buffalo extended the whole length of our afternoon's travel," emigrant William Kilgore wrote in his journal. "I estimated two million." Kilgore's estimate may have been an exaggeration, but he had a point.

The immense herds often blocked the path of the westward travelers. One wagon train, for example, had to wait for more than two hours as stampeding buffalo passed before it. Often during such a delay men would grab their rifles and take off on a buffalo hunt. Unlike the Native Americans who killed buffalo for their meat and used almost all the other parts of the animal, those pioneers who shot buffalo did so for the sport of it.

As one member of a wagon train, Isaac Foster, reported, "The valley of the Platte for 200 miles [is] dotted with skeletons of buffalo...every emigrant seems to wish to signalize himself by killing buffalo."

CHAPTER 4

Racing the Clock

"It is a glorious triumph for civilization and the Union. Settlements will follow the course of the road, and the East and West will be bound together by a chain of living Americans that can never be broken."

—President James Buchanan in a letter to the owner of the Butterfield Overland Mail, upon the stagecoach line's first run from San Francisco to St. Louis, 1858

As more settlers arrived on the western lands and established homes, farms, towns, and emerging cities, the need for communication and efficient transportation between settlements became paramount. Just as it had in the East, the stagecoach emerged as the most effective means of shrinking time and distance in the early West.

Wherever western settlement took place, stagecoach lines appeared. As early as the 1820s, almost a quarter century before the first great wagon trains headed deep into the West, regular stagecoach service was operating between budding communities along the Mississippi River. By the 1850s, 31 separate stagecoach lines had been established in Texas alone. In California the discovery of gold in 1849 and the immediate appearance of tens of thousands of gold-seekers led to the founding of the California Stage Company. By the 1860s, this one company operated 28 daily lines and employed 1,000 horses and 134 coaches, which carried passengers and mail across almost 2,000 miles of California roads.

The country's main stagecoach line was the Butterfield Overland Mail. Both settlers and government officials had talked about the benefits of a transcontinental stagecoach line that could carry both mail and passengers. In 1857, the U.S. government authorized such a line, mapping out a 2,795-mile, oxbow-shaped route between Memphis, Tennessee, and St. Louis, Missouri, to the East and San Francisco in the West. The contract for the line was awarded to John Butterfield, who had owned stagecoach lines in New York State. At the same time, he had owned and operated canal packets and lake steamboats and had also been involved in the building of some of the nation's earliest railroads.

Stagecoach passengers pose for the camera in a rare tranquil moment on their trip. The team of six horses indicates that theirs was a long journey, bound to be taken at breakneck speed.

His contract with the government required the Butterfield Overland Mail to deliver the mail from one end of the route to the other within 25 days. For this, the government paid the company $600,000 a year. Butterfield added to his revenue by charging passengers $100 for a one-way trip.

Butterfield's contract also called for him to use the highest-quality coaches pulled by the best four- or six-horse teams available. He bought 1,800 of the fastest and most dependable mustangs he could find and 250 new Concord coaches. He also hired the best stagecoach drivers he could corral and some 1,000 other employees, including station bosses, blacksmiths, veterinarians, and men to tend the horses at each relay station.

The Butterfield Overland Mail began operating on September 16, 1858. From the beginning, skeptics doubted that the line would ever be able to fulfill its contract by transporting mail, let alone passengers, over so long and difficult a route within 25 days. "Four-horse stages" wrote the *Sacramento Daily Union,* "cannot be driven from San Francisco, across the seven deserts...in twenty-five days—nor in forty days—nor at all. It never has been done. It never will be done."

The very first coach out of San Francisco arrived in St. Louis in just under 24 days. An excited Butterfield telegraphed the news to President James Buchanan. "I congratulate you upon the result," replied the President.

"It is a glorious triumph for civilization and the Union. Settlements will follow the course of the road, and the East and West will be bound together by a chain of living Americans that can never be broken."

In less than a decade—despite the hazards of searing heat in the desert, blizzards in the mountain passes, and endless open miles across the prairie—the time required for the trip was dramatically reduced. In 1864, one of Butterfield's coaches made the 2,000-mile trip from Folsom, California, to Atchison, Kansas, in 12 days and 2 hours.

Much of the success of the Butterfield Overland Mail was due to the skill and daring of the drivers. They knew their horses and how to get the most out of them. They developed, for example, the skill of descending the steepest grades at full gallop and of climbing the highest terrain at a well-controlled trot. Frightened yet thrilled passengers often shared the drivers' love of speed and sense of adventure. One English traveler, writing of the sensation of charging down a long mountainside at full speed, wrote that the

YELLOWSTONE–PARK

These 1890 travelers were journeying through Yellowstone, America's first national park. Even after railroads replaced many western stagecoach lines, in certain areas stages remained the best form of transportation.

experience was so exciting "that you cannot help cheering on the horses in spite of a very probable upset on the brow of an almost perpendicular rock several hundred feet in height." According to the traveler, even the horses seemed to take joy in the breakneck speed.

The glory days of the stagecoach in the West were relatively brief, however. By the 1860s, the railroad began to move into the western territories. It delivered faster and more comfortable service than any form of overland travel had ever provided. When the first of several transcontinental railroads was completed in 1869, the main role of the stagecoach became that of transporting passengers from one depot to another along the rapidly expanding railroad network. Still, it was the stagecoach that had largely made possible the rapid development of the early American West.

The saga of the West also included a much briefer story about a company of men and horses determined

This poster for the 1953 movie "Pony Express" highlights the skill and daring of the Pony Express riders. Nearly a century after they rode, their legendary exploits still captured the American imagination.

to make the delivery of mail even swifter than the fastest stagecoach could provide. The Pony Express was in existence for little more than a year and a half. But in that short time it provided an extraordinary service while earning a legendary place in the nation's history.

The private freighting company of Russell, Majors, and Waddell established the Pony Express. Its goal was to deliver mail along a more than 1,900-mile route that stretched from St. Joseph, Missouri, to Sacramento, California. Men would carry the mail on horseback night and day and ride in relays between stations set up at about 10-mile intervals along the route. The entire route was to be covered in just eight days.

It was an enormous undertaking. Hundreds of station keepers were hired, along with men to tend the horses at each stop. More than 120 daring and experienced riders were employed. The horses were chosen with even greater care. At a time when an average horse cost $40, the owners of the Pony Express paid up to $200 per animal to secure the very best. Many of these animals were mustangs that had been bred in California. Many others were horses known as three-quarter thoroughbreds. Still others were mixed breeds containing the blood of Morgans, quarter horses, and Indian horses. They all shared two common attributes: they were extremely fast and could be ridden at full gallop for many miles.

The Pony Express began operations on April 3, 1860. A rider started out from each end of the route. Each rode on a light saddle, which had a square leather pouch with pockets, called a *mochila,* secured to it. Inside the pockets, wrapped in oilskin, were about 20 pounds of mail.

A Pony Express rider usually covered about 100 miles in a day, stopping at each station along the route to mount a fresh horse. When his stint was over, he would gallop into a station and transfer the mail to the horse of a fresh rider, who would then race off toward the next station. The entire exchange took less than two minutes.

The Pony Express riders were extraordinary and fearless horsemen. The challenges they faced as they covered the long miles at a steady gallop would have broken the resolve of less courageous men. Mark Twain was one of their admirers. "No matter what time of the day or night [a Pony Express rider's] watch came on," he wrote,

and no matter whether it was winter or summer, raining, snowing, hailing, sleeting or whether his "beat" was a level straight road or a crazy trail over mountain crags and precipices, or whether it led through peaceful regions or regions that swarmed with hostile Indians, he must always be ready to leap into the saddle and be off with the wind.

Some of the individual feats became legendary. "Pony Bob" Halsam performed several. The speed record for covering the entire Pony Express route was established in March 1861, when riders carried copies of Abraham Lincoln's inaugural address to California in what was recorded as seven days and seven hours. During his stint in carrying the speech, Halsam rode eight hours without stopping and covered a distance of 120 miles. And he did it while traveling through country filled with hostile Indians.

Halsam accomplished his most remarkable feat, the one that gave him his nickname "Pony Bob," in the fall of 1860, during a time when the Paiute Indians were attacking white settlers in Nevada. After beginning his

A Pony Express rider flees from a hostile Native American. Despite such dangers, Pony Express riders covered a total of 650,000 miles and reportedly lost only one mail shipment.

trip, Halsam found that stations along the way had been temporarily abandoned out of fear of the Indians. He rode for 75 miles on the same horse before finally finding a station that was operating.

The rider at that station, who was supposed to complete the next leg of the journey, was scared of the Indians and refused to make the trip. Halsam rode on. He passed two other stations where riders also refused to relieve him. Pausing only to mount a fresh horse each time, Halsam continued on to yet another station where he was informed that he was the only rider available along the route to deliver the mail that was due

back at the station from which he had started. But he was now 185 miles away. Even though he had heard that Indian attacks were increasing, he kept going. Resting only for nine hours, he made the reverse journey, stopping only at stations where he was able to obtain a fresh horse. By the time he arrived back at his original starting point, he had traveled a grand total of 380 miles in some 27 hours.

When the first Pony Express riders raced along their route, they often passed workmen stringing telegraph wires on long poles. When, on October 24, 1861, telegraph connections between Kansas City and San Francisco were completed, bringing instant communication to the West, the days of the Pony Express came to an abrupt end.

CHAPTER 5

The Horse Helps Create a Legend

"A cow outfit is no better than its horses."

—Popular cowboy saying, around 1870

The Pony Express rider made his mark in an extremely short period of time. The glory days of another western figure, the cowboy, would also be brief, lasting little more than 20 years. Yet in these two decades the cowboy would become not only the West's most celebrated type but also the folk hero of a nation. And like the stagecoach and Pony Express riders, the cowboy relied on the horse to carry out his work.

In the years between 1866 and 1886, some 40,000 cowboys drove more than 9 million head of cattle from Texas, where they were raised, to railroad centers in Kansas some 500 miles north. From there, the cattle were shipped to slaughterhouses in Chicago, where they were killed and turned into the meat that fed the nation and much of the world. During that period, the beef industry grew so large that 1,365,000 square miles—44 percent of all the land in the United States—was devoted to cattle raising. The cowboy was at the center of this enormous venture.

Perhaps more books, plays, songs, movies, and television programs have been written about the cowboy than any other figure in popular American culture.

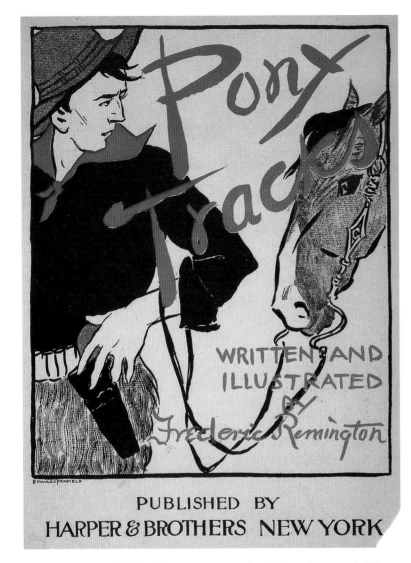

Originally published in 1895, Frederic Remington's illustrated book *Pony Tracks* includes a collection of magazine articles that he wrote about the West. Through his paintings, illustrations, and sculptures, Remington helped to make the cowboy an American hero.

Many of these depictions are romanticized, portraying the cowboy as a rugged individual in a stunning landscape. In reality, the cowboy was a tough, often lonely man with a hard job to do. And almost everything he did was on horseback.

The first cowboys were Mexicans called "vaqueros" (*vaca* is the Spanish word for "cow"). The early vaqueros tended the cattle on ranches operated either by wealthy Spanish landowners or by the Spanish Catholic church, which established ranches adjacent to many of their missions in Mexican territory. Throughout the 16th, 17th, and 18th centuries, the vaqueros tended these ranches, creating and perfecting the aspects of cattle raising that would come to mark the American cowboy's way of life.

Large-scale ranching began in the United States immediately after the end of the Civil War in 1865. Many of the American cowboys were veterans of that conflict. The type of clothes they wore, the equipment they used, the techniques they employed, even many of the terms they used in speaking were all taken in one

One vaquero aims to lasso a horse as his companions help to control the herd. Vaqueros "on foot," wrote cowboy artist Frederic Remington, "are odd fish. Their knees work outward and they have a decided hitch in their gait, but once let them get a foot in a stirrup and a grasp on the horn of a saddle, and a dynamite cartridge alone could expel them from their seat."

form or another from the vaqueros. Most important, the American cowboys acquired from the vaqueros their skill on horseback.

Like the cattle they tended, most of the cowboys' horses were descendants of the animals that the Spanish had brought to the New World. Over the centuries, these horses, like the cattle, had multiplied and roamed freely over the countryside. Cattle raising required the participation of scores of horses, and in the late spring cowboys captured wild horses and took them back to the ranch, where specially skilled cow-

men known as broncobusters carried out the difficult and dangerous job of taming them.

The life of the cowboy centered around three basic activities—tending the range, the roundup, and the cattle drive. Tending the range involved riding hundreds of miles to oversee the cattle as they roamed in search of the best grazing areas. One of the cowhand's main tasks was to keep the steers and calves from wandering onto neighboring spreads. He also had to prevent the cattle from feeding on poisonous bushes or drinking from any of the contaminated water holes that dotted the cattle country. Often the cowhands had to rescue animals that had fallen into gullies or managed to squeeze themselves between tall rocks.

The roundup was one of the highlights of the cowboy's year. Each spring, cowhands from various neighboring ranches spread out across the range and located the cattle that belonged to their ranch. They then drove the animals to a central location where the calves that had been born since the previous roundup were branded with the special mark of their ranch. Using a hot iron, a cowboy seared the brand into the calf's skin.

The work of the roundup required the skills of both the cowboys and the horses. The cowhands rode hundreds of miles locating the cattle and gathering the herds together. In order to do this, they needed three or four fresh mounts each day. In addition, the cowboys relied on specially trained horses to perform the demanding tasks of separating the calves to be branded from the herd, roping them, and dragging them to the branding area.

During the roundup, these horses were kept in a large roped-off corral called a "remuda," the Spanish word for "replacement." One of the ranch's youngest cowhands, called a wrangler, tended the horses in the remuda. His main job was to keep each horse fresh and ready when a cowboy selected it for a special task.

Separating the calves from the herd was perhaps the most demanding task. It was accomplished by using "cutting horses," which were trained to step gently so as not to excite the milling cattle. Once a cowboy astride a cutting horse located a calf to be separated from the herd, the horse worked itself between the targeted calf and the rest of the herd. As the frightened calf frantically tried to return to the herd, the cutting horse, trained literally to stop, start, and turn on a dime, kept moving the animal away from the rest of the cattle until it was completely clear of the herd and could be roped. A good cutting horse could accomplish this without any directions from its rider.

The job of securing the separated calves fell to other highly trained animals known as roping horses.

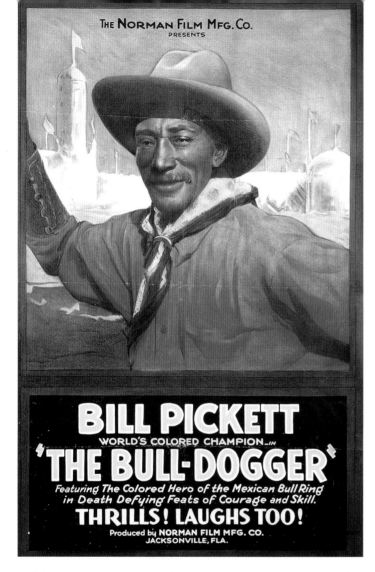

African-American cowboy Bill Pickett invented the technique called "bulldogging" in which he rode alongside a calf, dismounted, and immobilized the animal by biting it on its lower lip. A 1922 movie celebrated his exploits.

This animal was skilled at carrying a rider alongside a racing calf or steer and placing itself in the best position for the cowboy to throw a rope around the animal. Once the rope was secure, the roping horse came to an abrupt halt and planted its feet securely in the earth, holding the rope taut while its rider dismounted and threw the calf to the ground. With the help of other cowhands, the roper tied the calf's four feet together. The secured animal was then dragged to the branding pen.

All the work of the roundup was a prelude to the long trail drive, in which some 3,000 head of cattle would be driven hundreds of miles northward over one of several trails that led to the railroad yards.

Each cattle drive was a highly organized undertaking. In order to keep the cattle moving at a steady pace without straying, each cowboy rode in a designated place. At the front of the herd, the cook drove his horse-drawn vehicle, known as the chuck wagon, from which he prepared meals and fed the cowboys their breakfast, lunch, and dinner. The drive boss also rode at the head of the cattle, while other cowhands maintained positions at either side of the advancing herd.

Toward the back of the herd and off to one side, the wrangler led the remuda containing the various types of horses needed to complete the drive. The least experienced cowboys took positions at the rear of the pack, where they choked on the dust constantly kicked up by thousands of animals.

As in the roundup, the cattle drive required the use of a variety of specially skilled horses. Of these, the swimming horses were perhaps the most important. The long trails northward contained many rivers that had to be crossed, always a dangerous maneuver. Swimming horses were trained to find the safest place to lead the herd across a river. The cattle, afraid of water, were easily spooked, but the swimming horses had the ability to coax them into the river, keep them moving, and lead them to the opposite bank.

A trail drive could take as long as three months to complete. Once it was over and the cattle were herded onto waiting railroad cars, the cowboys were free to "relax" in one of the many rowdy towns that grew up alongside the railroad centers. When their carousing was over, many of the cowhands returned to the cattle country, where the yearly cycle of range tending, roundup, and trail drive was repeated.

As with the stagecoach and Pony Express riders, technological advances brought the heyday of the cowboy to an end. By the late 1880s, the railroad had made its way into cattle country, making it possible to ship the herds directly from the range to the slaughterhouses. The long cattle drive became unnecessary. Two other factors also played a role in altering the life the cowboys had known. As millions of settlers arrived in the West, they fenced in the open range that had been at the heart of large-scale cattle raising. And in 1886, the severest winter in its history hit the cattle country. As hurricane-force winds swept the prairies and temperatures plummeted to $-20°$ F, hundreds of thousands of cattle froze to death. It was the final blow to raising cattle on the range, one of the most colorful chapters in the nation's history.

The cowboy's main duty was tending cattle, and he was expected to do it in every type of weather. Fierce blizzards made the work particularly hard.

CHAPTER 6

Omnibuses and Horsecars

"Modern martyrdom may be succinctly defined as riding

in a New York omnibus."

—*New York Herald*, 1835

From 1840 to 1890, so many people settled out West that in 1890 the federal government said that the region could no longer be classified as a frontier. From 1860 to 1910, despite the fact that millions of settlers had left the cities, these urban centers, with their entertainment, shopping, and work opportunities, continued to grow at a phenomenal rate. In 1860, only one American in four lived in a city. By 1890, one in three did. And by 1910, nearly half of all Americans lived in a city. And just as the horse was essential to life in the West, it dominated the nation's urban areas as well.

American cities teemed with horses. Private citizens rode to and from work and carried out their errands on horseback. Many policemen patrolled their beats astride their mounts. Horse-drawn delivery wagons, peddlers' carts, fire engines, ambulances, cabs, and private carriages clogged the city streets. Every well-to-do residence had its own stable and carriage house. Public stables, blacksmith shops, hitching posts, and watering troughs abounded.

From the time that cities began to grow, inhabitants needed some form of public transportation. The earliest

The appearance first of omnibuses and then of horsecars revolutionized transportation within American cities. Horsedrawn vehicles created New York's first traffic jams in the 1830s.

solution was a horse-drawn vehicle called an omnibus. First used in London and Paris, the omnibus made its initial American appearance in New York City in 1831. By 1844, Philadelphia, Boston, and Baltimore all had their own bustling omnibus lines. The omnibus became so popular that in New York one of these passenger-filled vehicles made its way past City Hall every 15 seconds.

The earliest omnibuses resembled stagecoaches. But soon, longer and narrower vehicles were built, which made them look more like modern buses. Teams of two to six horses pulled them. The word "Omnibus" was written on each side of the vehicle. Borrowing from the stagecoach, omnibuses were decorated with brightly painted scenes on their sides. Fringed curtains adorned their windows.

An official (far right) from the American Society for the Prevention of Cruelty to Animals (ASPCA) checks the condition of an overworked horse. The heavy loads and the demand for speed weakened or injured many of the horses that pulled horsecars. In part to remedy this situation, concerned citizens formed the ASPCA in 1866.

Traveling on an omnibus was far from an enjoyable experience, however. The buses were always overcrowded with passengers who bumped into each other and stepped on each other's feet. Many of the early city streets were paved with cobblestones, and riders were jarred and thrown about as the buses moved along the uneven surfaces. "The arrangements for shooting passengers out into the mud are unsurpassed," wrote the *New York Tribune.* In addition, the harried drivers were often surly, and quarrels with passengers were common.

Even more serious was the danger the omnibus presented to other city traffic. As drivers from rival companies raced across city streets in order to beat each other to waiting passengers, private carriages, delivery wagons, and pedestrians were apt to get caught between them, causing injury and even death. "A ferocious spirit," wrote yet another newspaper, "appears to have taken possession of the drivers, which defies law and delights in destruction."

As omnibus travel became increasingly popular and yet more difficult and dangerous, transit owners began to search for a more comfortable and less hazardous way of moving people around the city. They found their inspiration in the earliest railroads, which, in 1830, were just being developed. Rails provided a far smoother ride than did rough street surfaces. Traveling over rails also meant the route was set, rather than haphazard, as it was with the omnibuses.

From this example set by the railroads emerged the horsecar, an omnibus-type vehicle pulled by horses over rails set into city streets. John Mason, one of New York's wealthiest citizens, established the first horsecar line in the United States. Mason hired stagecoach builder John Stephenson to design and construct his horsecars, which were highly decorated and featured cast-iron wheels. "They resemble an omnibus, or rather several omnibuses attached to each other," reported the *Morning Courier,* "padded with fine cloth and with handsome glass windows, each capable of containing outside and inside fully forty passengers."

The first run on Mason's line, which he named the New York and Harlem Railroad, occurred on November 14, 1832, before a large group of spectators. The *New York Enquirer* reported:

> Officials of The New York and Harlem Railroad with Mayor Walter Browne and others of distinction left the City Hall in carriages to deposit near Union Square where two splendid cars, each with two horses, were in waiting. The company was soon seated and the horses trotted off in handsome style, with great ease, at the rate of about 12 miles, followed by a group of private [carriages] and horsemen. Groups of spectators greeted the passengers of the cars with shouts and every window in the Bowery was filled.

This initial horsecar trip so impressed Mayor Browne that upon its completion he stated, "This event will go down in history as the greatest achievement of man." It was, of course, an exaggeration but also an indication of the widespread acceptance that the horsecar would quickly gain. By 1835, a horsecar line had been established in New Orleans. In the early 1850s, other lines were operating in New York City.

By 1859, the vehicles filled the streets of such cities as Boston, Chicago, Philadelphia, Denver, Baltimore,

FINEST IN THE WORLD.

R.B. CROUCH, Chicago.

kept their lines operating long after the horsecars appeared, complained that horsecar tracks obstructed the movement of their buses. Drivers of delivery wagons and other horse-drawn conveyances were also upset. Private citizens who daily traveled the city streets on horseback added their voices to the protests.

and Cleveland. A report issued in 1881 proclaimed that 415 horsecar lines, consisting of some 3,000 miles of track, were flourishing throughout the United States. More than 100,000 horses pulled the 18,000 cars involved in these operations.

The horsecar lines created a new problem for the other vehicles. Omnibus operators, many of whom

The tracks caused many injuries and deaths to both animals and humans when horses slid on the slippery tracks or caught their hooves between the rails. Outraged drivers sometimes deliberately brought their horses to a halt across the tracks to block the path of the horsecar. Many accidents resulted. "In New York

City they kill one person each week on city railroads and mangle three or four on an average in the same space of time. Human life is really of little value these days," stated the *New York Sunday Dispatch.*

Nevertheless, horsecars continued to attract a growing number of passengers. More horses were needed to keep the lines moving along. Companies carefully selected these horses. The age of the animals was a prime factor. Most companies avoided using young horses because they were too frisky to pull the cars along at a steady pace. And they avoided older horses because it was difficult to change their ways and teach them to make smooth stops and starts and to remain unfazed in the midst of the tumultuous city traffic—skills vital to horsecar hauling. Also, many companies used only gray horses, convinced that they could withstand summer heat better than animals of a different color.

In 1892, when American photographer Alfred Stieglitz took this photograph, horsecars still operated throughout the nation. To Stieglitz and thousands of New Yorkers, the horsecar was a vital symbol of city life.

Because the horses were by far the most expensive part of any horsecar operation, they were treated with care. Fresh animals took over every four or five hours. Back in the stable, they were groomed, watered, and fed hay and grain three times a day, along with treats such as oats and carrots. In all, they ate about 30 pounds of food every day. Every horsecar stable employed its own veterinarian, who kept the animals healthy.

Although the omnibus and the horsecar were the most common means of urban public transportation, there was another, less crowded, considerably more expensive way to move about the city. This was a hansom cab, what we would today call a taxi.

The use of hansom cabs dates back to Paris in the late 1600s. There, an enterprising Frenchman named Nicholas Savage began charging people a modest fare to transport them from one place to another. Hansom cabs first appeared in the United States in 1829 when Ephraim Dodge established a cab service between Boston and South Boston. A ride cost 12 1/2 cents.

By the 1840s, hansom cabs operated in many American cities, but they were most common in Boston and New York. This vehicle was a light, usually elegantly appointed buggy-type conveyance. It was so light, in fact, that a passenger had to climb aboard carefully to keep the cab from tipping over. A single horse, meticulously groomed, pulled the cab. Wealthy citizens used hansom cabs most often, because they were much more expensive to ride in than omnibuses or horsecars. A young man, out on a date, might splurge on a cab ride in order to impress his companion.

The heyday of the hansom cab has long since passed. But in many cities, such as Charleston, South Carolina, Savannah, Georgia, New York, and Boston, there are still horsedrawn carriages in operation that provide sightseers and fun-seekers with leisurely trips through parks, to historic sites, and to other places of interest. Many people ride in them to get a sense of what it was like to travel in an age gone by.

The hansom cab was named after its inventor, Joseph A. Hansom. With leather and brass trim they were among the most elegantly outfitted of all the horse-drawn vehicles.

CHAPTER 7
The Horse Delivers the Goods

"It is an endless parade, this never-ending procession of horses and wagons plodding to and from the ships. If you like horses…go down to the docks. But be warned. The horse traffic leaves little room for human perambulation."

—*San Francisco Examiner*, 1898

Not only people moved about the city by horse. Horse-drawn vehicles transported almost all goods, and freight wagons of almost every description clogged the cities. Most of the nation's growing factories were located within these urban centers, and they required enormous amounts of raw materials to manufacture their products. Teams of powerful horses hauled the wagons that delivered the materials and manufacturing machinery. These wagons made their way daily through the city and lined up in front of the factories' receiving platforms, waiting to be unloaded. There men loaded other horsedrawn wagons with finished goods to be hauled to nearby towns and cities.

Horse and wagon took much of the raw material from ships that lined the docks of the nation's seaports to its factories. Tons of finished goods were, in turn, hauled to the docks and shipped to other ports around the nation and throughout the world.

As the cities continued to grow, more materials were required for the construction of office buildings, stores, and homes. Horse-drawn freight wagons, filled with lumber and bricks, poured through the city

The cities required tons of different kinds of goods to keep them operating, and horses delivered almost all of them. One of the most important of these goods was coal, used not only to fuel a city's factories, businesses, and stores, but also essential for heating the nation's homes.

streets. Added to all this traffic were the thousands of delivery wagons that supplied the stores with their goods. At a time when shops commonly delivered groceries, hardware, clothing, and other products directly to the customer, almost every establishment had its own delivery wagon and horses. Contributing to the confusion of omnibuses, horsecars, hacks, private coaches, and freight and delivery wagons were peddlers and farmers from the surrounding countryside, who sold their wares and produce directly from their carts and wagons.

The presence of so many horses also caused a problem that went beyond urban congestion. Every year the horses dropped tons of manure. Aside from the bad smell, it presented a real challenge to pedestrians as they tried to maneuver their way across city streets.

Even more serious, the manure attracted flies and other disease-transmitting insects.

In addition to these challenges of city life, the clip-clopping of all the horses and the sound of the iron wheels created an incessant noise. To many, the sound was almost deafening.

Some cities, in an attempt to control the racket, passed laws prohibiting wagons drawn by more than four horses from entering the city. It became a common practice to lay out straw in front of a sick person's house in order to keep down the noise. Boston and a few other cities made it illegal for horse-drawn traffic to pass by their courthouses, so that lawyers and witnesses could be heard. Many city doctors claimed that the endless noise of horses and the vehicles they pulled was the cause of a growing number of "nervous diseases."

However, not every noise created by horse traffic was unwelcome. Until well into the 20th century, most

A GLIMPSE OF NEW YORK'S DRY GOODS DISTRICT
The Largest in the World.   Covering a Space of 135 Acres.   Containing 4,600 Firms.   Employing $800,000,000 Capital.

Well into the 1900s horses, many of them pulling loaded wagons, dominated the streets of American cities. In urban centers such as New York, Boston, Chicago, and Philadelphia simply getting across a major thoroughfare presented a serious challenge to pedestrians.

city buildings and houses were made primarily of wood. Hundreds of structures caught fire every year. Fighting fires was a major, often heroic effort, and firefighters depended upon horses.

Every city fire-fighting brigade kept a team of horses in special stalls within the firehouse. Fire horses had to be fast, agile, and smart. They also had to be strong. Fire wagons, containing all the equipment needed to put out a conflagration, weighed as much as 4,000 pounds. Whether they pulled a wagon with ladders and hoses or one containing either hand or steam pumpers, the horses had to be able to race from the station, haul the wagons through the dense city traffic, and get the firemen to their destination without mishap as quickly as possible. Not only property but lives depended upon the horses' strength and skill.

Three-horse teams pulled most fire wagons, although two horses were sometimes used to haul lighter equipment. The horses were usually medium in size and were almost always perfectly matched. All were carefully selected and highly trained to ensure that they were as responsive to a fire alarm as the human firefighters were.

When the alarm bell in the firehouse sounded, the horses, without any direction from the firemen, immediately left the open stalls and moved quickly in front of the fire wagon. Ropes on the ceiling suspended harnesses above the horses. With a tug of the reins, a fireman would lower the harnesses into place, and secure them. Within two minutes from the time the alarm sounded, the station doors would be open and horses and men would be charging out into the street.

The horses were the pride and joy not only of the firemen but of the people who lived in the neighborhood. Locals paid daily visits to the station to pet the horses, feed them lumps of sugar, carrots, and other treats, and even teach them tricks.

Fighting fires with horses was so effective and so admired that well after the truck was invented and motorized fire engines made their appearance, many cities and towns were reluctant to give up their horse-drawn equipment. When the last team of fire horses in

Young boys in New Haven, Connecticut, race alongside
horses galloping to a fire. As late as 1915, horses still
pulled much of the nation's firefighting equipment.

New York City made its final run in 1922, thousands of people lined the streets to get one last look at the sight. Eight years later, 50,000 spectators gathered in Detroit to bid farewell as that city's last horse-drawn fire brigade made its final dash through the streets.

Until the early 1900s, thousands of police officers in the United States performed their duty on horseback. With the invention of the automobile, cars, trucks, and buses replaced almost all the horses. Although horses do not play the essential role that they once did in American cities, in one area they still perform a vital service. In the 1960s and 70s, many cities reinstated mounted patrol units after discovering that they were sometimes more effective than patrol cars.

The triangular patch worn by all members of the New York City Mounted Unit distinguishes them from their fellow police officers. It is sewn on the left sleeve of their uniforms.

Ed Cahill is a retired member of Boston's Mounted Police Unit and a strong believer in the use of police horses. "The elevated position of a mounted police officer," says Cahill,

makes him six times more visible and helps him to spot and deter certain types of crimes like mugging, purse snatching and auto thefts. There is no question that a policeman on a horse is more approachable and less isolated from the neighborhood than a policeman in a cruiser. Neighborhood residents feel good about a policeman on a horse. It puts the police back in touch with the neighborhoods that they are responsible to protect.

Certain animals, such as a Boston police horse named Prescott, have become neighborhood favorites. For more than 20 years Prescott has performed so well that he has earned the name "the wonder horse." "The horse has paid his dues over and over—riots, strikes, parades, the marathon—he's done it all," says Boston mounted patrolman Emilio Cirello. "But that's only half of it. Prescott has made horsemen out of dozens of rookie riders."

Prescott is getting up in age, so Cirello and his fellow mounted officers have prepared for the sad day when the horse passes away by reserving a plot for him in a popular pet cemetery. "If I thought there was some way we could finance it," states Cirello, "I'd like to erect a statue of a horse and policeman at that grave."

Cirello's desire to honor Prescott is most fitting. It reflects the way millions of Americans throughout our history have felt about their four-legged companions and helpmates. No understanding of U.S. history can be complete without an appreciation of what it owes to the horse.

Boston mounted police officers pose atop their four-legged crime fighters. Members of the nation's mounted police units carry on a tradition established by the country's very first police forces.

Timeline

8000 BC
North American horses die out

1492
Christopher Columbus brings horses to Caribbean

1519
Spanish explorer Hernán Cortés reintroduces horses to North American mainland

1520
Spaniards introduce North American Indians to horse

1600–50
Spanish missions in California and Texas spread horses northward

1600–1860
Spanish cowboys called "vaqueros" tend mission ranches and establish cattle-raising procedures

1630–1750
European colonists bring thousands of horses to East Coast

1717
Conestoga wagons first built

1800–25
Turnpikes built nationwide

1800–50
Conestoga wagons become popular way to move freight

around 1825
Regular stagecoach service established

1827
Abbot, Downing Company of Concord, New Hampshire builds first Concord Coach

1831
First omnibus line established

1832
First horsecar line established

1840s–70s
Thousands of families make their way West in covered wagons

1840s
Hansom cabs operate in major cities Stagecoach lines run on regular schedules throughout East

1858
Butterfield Overland Mail begins operations

1860
Pony Express begins operations

1861
Telegraph kills Pony Express

1864
More than 8,000 wagon trains pass through Omaha, Nebraska in one day

1866–86
Some 40,000 cowboys raise and tend more than 9 million head of cattle and drive them to railway centers some 500 miles north of cattle country

1870–90
Aided by horse-drawn machinery, tens of thousands of prairie farmers feed nation and world

1908
Henry Ford begins mass production of automobiles

1915
U.S. horse population peaks at 21.5 million head

1922
Last team of New York City fire horses makes its final run

1925–50
Number of machine-hauling horses on farms drops from more than 100,000 to less than 2,000

1950–2002
Horsedrawn carriages tourist attractions in many cities

1975–2002
Mounted units help prevent crime

Places to Visit

The following museums contain excellent collections of art and artifacts relating to the history of the horse in America. Almost all have a web site providing specific information about the museum, such as visiting hours and directions on how to get there.

Arizona

Phippen Museum of Western Art
4701 North US Highway 89
Prescott, AZ 86301
www.phippenartmuseum.org

Colorado

Pro Rodeo Hall of Fame and Museum
of the American Cowboy
101 ProRodeo Drive
Colorado Springs, CO 80919
www.prorodeo.com/PRHOF

Florida

Gloria Austin Carriage Museum
Florida Carriage Driving Center
Continental Acres Equine Resort
3000 Marion County Road
Weirsdale, FL 32195
www.austineducationcenter.com

Idaho

Appaloosa Museum and Heritage
Center
2720 W. Pullman Road
Moscow, ID 83843
www.appaloosamuseum.org

Kentucky

The International Museum of the
Horse at the Kentucky Horse Park
4089 Iron Works Parkway
Lexington, KY 40511
www.imh.org

Missouri

Patee House Museum
12th and Penn Streets
St. Joseph, MO 64502
http://members.tripod.com/~
mogmios/stjoseph_history/

New Mexico

Institute of American Indian Arts
Museum
108 Cathedral Place
Santa Fe, NM 87501
www.iaiancad.org/museum.htm

Oklahoma

Gilcrease Museum
1400 North Gilcrease Museum Road
Tulsa, OK 74127
www.gilcrease.org

Museum of the Great Plains
601 NW Ferris Avenue
Lawton, OK 73507
www.museumgreatplains.org

Pennsylvania

Carriage Museum of America
Bird-In-Hand, PA 17505
www.carriagemuseumlibrary.org

Texas

American Quarter Horse Heritage
Center and Museum
2601 I-40 East at Quarter Horse Drive
Amarillo, TX 79104
www.aqha.com/horse/museum

Vermont

The Justin Morgan Memorial
    Museum
3 Bostwick Road
Shelburne, VT 05482
www.uvm.edu/~histpres/vtiana/
    morgan.html

Virginia

Carriage Museum of America
Morven Park Route 3
Leesburg, VA 20176

Wyoming

Buffalo Bill Historical Center
720 Sheridan Avenue
Cody, WY 82414
www.bbhc.org

Further Reading

Appelt, Kathi. *Down Cut Shin Creek: The Pack Horse Librarians of Kentucky.* New York: Harpercollins Juvenile Books, 2001.

Bourne, Russell. *Americans on the Move.* Golden, Colo.: Fulcrum, 1995.

Braider, Donald. *The Life, History, and Magic of the Horse.* New York: Grosset & Dunlap, 1973.

Dossenbach, Monique and Hans Dossenbach. *The Noble Horse.* Boston: G.K. Hall, 1983.

Jurmain, Suzanne. *Once Upon a Horse: A History of Horses—And How They Shaped Our History.* New York: Lothrop, Lee & Shepard, 1989.

Mitchell, Edwin. *Horse and Buggy Age in New England.* Detroit: Gale, 1974.

Peterson, Cris. *Horsepower: The Wonder of Draft Horses.* Boyds Mills, 1997.

Sandler, Martin W. *The Vaqueros: America's First Cowmen.* New York: Holt, 2001.

Sandler, Martin W. *This Was America.* Boston: Little Brown, 1980.

Viola, Herman J. *After Columbus: The Horse's Return to America.* Norwalk, Conn.: Soundprints, 1992.

Index

Page numbers in **bold** indicate illustrations.

Martin W. Sandler is the author of more than 40 books. His *Story of American Photography: An Illustrated History for Young People* received the Horn Book Award in 1984. Sandler's other books include *America, A Celebration!, Photography: An Illustrated History, The Vaqueros: The World's First Cowmen,* and the Library of Congress American History series for young adults. An accomplished television producer and writer as well, Sandler has received Emmy and Golden Cine awards for his television series and programs on history, photography, and American business. He has taught American Studies to students in junior high and high school, as well as at the University of Massachusetts and Smith College. He lives in Cotuit, Massachusetts, with his wife Carol.

Other titles in the Transportation in America series include:

On the Waters of the USA: Ships and Boats in American Life

Riding the Rails in the USA: Trains in American Life

Straphanging in the USA: Trolleys and Subways in American Life

Driving around the USA: Automobiles in American Life

Flying over the USA: Airplanes in American Life